SELT
1 & 2 Conqueror Court
Velum Drive
Sittingbourne
Kent
ME10 5BH

www.selt.org.uk

© Debbie Robins and John West-Burnham 2011

All rights reserved. No part of this publication may be reproduced or transmitted in any form or by any means, electronic or mechanical, including photocopying, recording, or any information storage or retrieval system, without prior permission in writing from the publishers.
ISBN: 978-0-9566679-4-6

Printed and bound by Heronswood Press Limited

Leadership for Collaboration

Debbie Robins and John West-Burnham

Contents   **Page**

	Introduction	4
1.	Case study: high level collaboration in a cluster of primary schools	7
2.	The case for collaboration	12
3.	Barriers to collaborative working	18
4.	Models of collaboration	24
5.	Strategies for effective collaboration	30
6.	Conclusion: leadership for collaboration	44

Introduction

Easter Island is one of the remotest places on the planet. It is an island of 66 square miles and for much of its history was, like most Pacific islands, intensely forested. At its peak the population of the island was probably about 15,000. What Easter Island is best known for are, of course, the gigantic stone statues, the moai. How a society with no metal implements, no wheels and only human power carved, moved and erected these massive sculptures (some weighing over 80 tons) is one of the great mysteries of human civilization. An equal mystery is the fact that when Easter Island was 'discovered' by Europeans in 1722 it was virtually treeless; the population was about 10 per cent of its maximum; enormous sea bird populations had been wiped out and the moai were no longer being built. What had happened?

It seems that the demands of building the moai came to dominate every aspect of Easter Island society. In particular there is very clear evidence that over time the statues grew in size and complexity and this is probably best explained by competition between the various clans on the island; not so much an arms race as a statue race. The archaeological evidence points to a long period of sharing resources across the island and then increasing competition that accelerated the decline of an already fragile ecology. What is very clear is that the increasing competition led to deforestation that in turn led to increasing difficulty in growing traditional crops which in turn led to competition for increasingly scarce resources which in turn led to a form of civil war. The population collapsed, the rival factions destroyed the moai largely because the pressure to compete was more powerful than the pressure to survive, and Easter Island effectively died as a natural, social and cultural environment because of the failure to collaborate.

In his analysis of the collapse of society in Easter Island, Jared Diamond concludes:

> That leaves us with just two main sets of factors behind Easter's collapse: human environmental impacts, especially deforestation . . . and the political, social and religious factors behind the impacts . . . competition between clans and chiefs driving the erection of bigger statues requiring more wood, rope and food. (Diamond 2005:118)

At a time when collaboration was the only way to possibly solve the problems of the island, competition became the prevailing culture. Diamond draws a powerful conclusion from the fate of Easter Island:

> The parallels between Easter Island and the whole modern world are chillingly obvious . . . all countries on Earth today share resources and affect each other, just as did Easter's dozen clans. (Ibid: 119)

From his subsequent discussion of the collapse of a Norse settlement in medieval Greenland, Diamond draws another significant lesson:

> The Norse were undone by the same social glue that had enabled them to master Greenland's difficulties. That proves to be a common theme throughout history and also in the modern world . . . the values to which people cling most stubbornly under inappropriate conditions are those values that were previously the source of their greatest triumphs over adversity. (Ibid: 275)

The same might be said of education and children's services.

The purpose of this resource is to help identify the values, behaviours, skills, policies and strategies that will support the movement towards greater collaboration between schools. We do not underestimate the challenge involved in this movement. Although naturally social, and probably at their very best in social environments, human beings do seem to have a predisposition to compete and to become insular and exclusive. Whether in the banal simplicity of the pub quiz, the local football team, the testosterone driven world of high finance or the catastrophe of war human beings seem to need to compete. In fact competition seems to be the basis for collaboration in many cases – we overcome our insularity in order to be better at competing.

The tension between the individualistic and collaborative imperatives is very strong. Hence the perceived power of the market as a key motivating force in human development, the centrality of competitive games to most cultures and a very strong individualistic streak in western societies. Buonfino and Mulgan (2006:1) use the powerful image of Porcupines in winter offered by Schopenhauer:

> On a cold winter's day, a group of porcupines huddled together to stay warm and keep from freezing. But, soon, they felt one another's quills and moved apart. When the need for warmth brought them closer together again, their quills again forced them apart. They were driven back and forth at the mercy of their discomforts until they found the distance from one another that provided both a maximum of warmth and a minimum of pain.

This, in essence, is the heart of this study – how to find the balance between personal space and optimum collaboration for mutual benefit. The first section of this resource is a detailed case study of a high level of collaboration between a cluster of primary schools - in many ways it is a microcosm for all of the issues that we explore and discuss in this resource. This first case study provides the structure for the rest of this resource. Chapter 2 explores the case for collaboration from a number of perspectives – from government policy to moral leadership and the antithesis of these perspectives is explored in chapter

3. Chapter 4 offers an overview of the many different approaches to collaboration and it is followed by an examination of the strategies most likely to support, develop and sustain collaborative working. The final chapter is a short summary of the key principles that have emerged in the course of developing this resource.

CHAPTER 1.
Case study: high-level collaboration in a cluster of primary schools

Context

This is an account of seven primary schools in south east England collaborating since 2005 to develop leadership capacity across all schools in a network that worked as an informal and voluntary partnership. The network initially consisted of 7 schools led by head teachers who wanted to support school improvement through a model of peer review. The group, formed in 2005, were self-selected; sharing a commitment to developing peer-led self-evaluation to extend the school's own processes. As the network developed, the opportunities to develop leadership capacity across the schools through distributing responsibility for leading the process became increasingly evident and this led to leadership development becoming as important a driver for the group as the original focus on self evaluation.

The initial model

In the first year of the network's development a model was established which consisted of taking teams of up to eight teachers into a partner school, reviewing an aspect of provision in order to confirm or challenge the host school's own view of its performance.

An initial planning meeting took place between head teachers and deputies in each pairing to identify the focus of the visit and the expertise required from the visiting team. This was followed by a two day visit involving teachers with significant leadership experience in their own school who undertook classroom observations, engaged in learning conversations with staff and interviews with pupils, parents and, on occasion, governors. The team also included a small group of children who contributed a child's perspective to the review. Verbal feedback was given to the host school at the end of the visit and this was followed by a written review report which formed a key evidence source for the school's own self evaluation.

Overcoming initial challenges

During the first year heads and deputies led the process. Teachers invited to be part of the review teams had considerable existing experience of observing teaching and learning and of giving feedback in their own schools. This was felt to be very important given the high level of expertise involved in undertaking such a role in another organisation. Considerable effort was made by the head teacher steering group to minimise an 'Ofsted' approach to the reviews and this included providing network coaching training for all visit team leaders to ensure consistency of approach. A protocol for visits was created, with input from team leaders, to give clear guidance on conducting reviews. In addition, the steering group of heads and deputies organised a launch conference for all teachers in the seven schools with a guest speaker, at which all head teachers shared the vision for the network and the benefits of collaboration.

The steering group held regular meetings during the first year, partly to establish the model and constantly review progress, but also crucially, to continue to build trust between all participating head teachers and deputies. Some of the members of the group had existing established professional relationships, others had never met prior to the creation of the network and opportunities were actively sought to develop high levels of professional trust, including regular lunch meetings, social events and the introduction of a two day residential review at the end of the round of visits.

The case for distributed leadership

At the end of the first round of visits senior teacher team leaders met to review the process from their perspective. This review was facilitated by one of the head teachers who was also an experienced facilitator with the National College. The finding of the review fed into the evaluation of the process by the steering group and ultimately to any changes identified for the next round. This evaluation model continued and is still in operation. As a result of the findings it was agreed that head teachers and deputies would play an advisory role only in the next round, allowing teachers with a range of prior experience to lead the visits.
A coaching model was introduced to support those new to leading review teams and head teachers played a key role in ensuring that the next generation of team leaders were provided with both practical and developmental support. Over the next three years the model continued with increasingly less experienced teachers taking a leading role in the review visits. Their development continued to be supported through coaching from steering group members in their own school as well as the regular final review meeting facilitated by the head teacher acting as lead facilitator. In addition, head teachers supporting newly emerging term leaders development ensured each team always included a teacher who had previously led a visit to act as mentor.

By the third year, teaching assistants were playing an increasingly significant role in the review visits and the designated lead network member now established in each school supported their learning. Notably, by this point, this was unlikely to be a member of the Senior Leadership team. During the review cycle 2008-9 one review visit was led by a teaching assistant, coached by a teacher with no formal leadership responsibilities. Both of them grew significantly in leadership confidence during the process.

Sustainability

During the five-year life of the network there have been challenges to its continuation. Most notably, these have been when member schools underwent a change of head teacher. In year two, one of the steering group heads retired and their successor did not include the network in their vision for moving the school forward. This served as a steep learning curve for remaining steering group head teachers as, having agreed with Governors that sympathy to the philosophy of the collaborative network would be a feature of all member school's succession planning, and having invested time in inducting the new head teacher, the colleague still chose to leave the group. It is clear that a total commitment from the head of each school was essential for continuation in the group.

A second school reluctantly left the group when the head undertook an Executive role as part of a planned federation with another local school, leaving both him and his leadership team with limited capacity in the short term to contribute effectively to the network.

An additional school joined the network, having being invited by an existing steering group member and the decision being validated by the whole group. Significant investment in induction of the new school's leadership team has resulted in the school being able to play a full part in their first round of visits. In addition, one of the founder head teachers, having been seconded to several interim headships elsewhere in the county eventually resigned from the original school. The school's deputy took on the role of acting head and was supported by the network steering group members during a period of significant challenge for the school. A further school has recently been invited to join the network as the head teachers, remaining resolutely committed to the positive outcomes of collaborative working, continuing to adapt and redefine the functioning of the network as circumstances demand.

Sustainability has been very much a matter of developing a broadly based level of involvement using the idea of distributed leadership as the basis for increasing involvement. The network has also been assiduous in supporting and developing members and this has helped to embed sustainable approaches.

Outcomes and impact
The initial rationale for the network; to promote school improvement through collaborative peer review has had a clear and positive impact as measured by the increasing effectiveness of partner school's self review processes as validated by Ofsted inspections, many of which specifically noted the impact of the network. School improvement outcomes, again as evidenced by Ofsted, show only two out of the original seven schools maintained a satisfactory grading, (one of which left in the second year), with two now being judged good and three outstanding.

There has also been an identifiable impact on the development of practice across the network schools with many examples of sharing aspects of provision working well, much of which has contributed to significant improvements in attainment. Examples include sharing effective practice in developing writing, developing effective behaviour management, improving SEN support and the development of Learning Platforms. The introduction by the steering group heads of an annual whole network conference with significant keynote speakers and structured opportunities to learn with colleagues from partner schools throughout the day has been important here. The conferences have included all members of   staff including admin teams and premises staff. Head teachers have facilitated the development of focus groups who meet termly including NQTs, some subject leaders, librarians and admin officers, ensuring the collaborative learning opportunities are available to all staff.

A further positive outcome has been the role of the network in providing peer support for steering group head teachers and deputies. The high levels of trust and the experience of participating in mutual projects over a significant period of time have created a natural support network for the senior leaders of all partner schools. Colleagues experiencing periods of challenge have gravitated to the close knit group and those moving from deputy to headship roles within the schools have found natural mentoring and coaching opportunities which, they have all identified as being of crucial importance.

The most significant outcome has been on the development of leadership capacity across the network of schools enabled by the explicit strategy of steering group head teachers. A National College Research Associate Report undertaken by three steering group heads identified significant leadership learning in groups of existing experienced leaders, middle leaders and inexperienced teachers, all of whom had opportunities over time to take a leading role in the design and implementation of visits. All groups described being taken out of their 'comfort zone' and finding they were capable of far more than they initially thought. A number of staff have been able to develop their careers; three senior teachers or deputies are now head teachers, two middle leaders are now deputies and three are undertaking acting deputy roles. A large group of initially inexperienced teachers are now taking active leadership roles both within their own schools and across the network, including facilitating focus groups.

Significantly, the network has grown a generation of new leaders who are morally committed to collaborative working. They have benefited from structured opportunities to develop effective collaborative leadership skills through personal experience, coaching and working alongside strong role models. They demonstrate an understanding of a lateral rather than the hierarchical leadership style required for effective collaboration. This is in stark contrast to the apparent understanding of many peer emergent leaders, and those already in post who are the product of the competitive environment of recent years and who see collaboration over competition as a considerable challenge. This is perhaps the most significant legacy of the network and one that is set to continue, particularly as these emerging leaders increasingly move to senior posts in other schools.

Implications for leadership for collaboration

The success of the network is attributable to a range of factors:
- A strong moral purpose for collaboration with school leaders committed to improving outcomes for children beyond their own school.
- Steering group heads and deputies articulating the vision for the collaboration, drawing explicitly on moral drivers and organising a range of activities to underpin this such as annual shared network conferences with inspirational speakers and the development of an increasing range of focus groups.
- A real commitment to distributed leadership as being the key to effective collaboration and a willingness to 'step back' from the process while providing appropriate support for those 'stepping up' to the challenge.
- Actively deploying a coaching model across the network to support the development of leadership capacity. This included head teachers supporting emergent leaders in partner schools as well as their own.
- A commitment to the induction of schools and staff new to the group including an annual training session on the history and rationale for the network for all newly appointed staff across the schools.
- Ensuring appropriate and sustainable structures were in place across all schools so that network activities were anchored into each school's culture. This included including network development in each school's improvement plan and ensuring funding was in place to support planned activities.
- A commitment to continually reviewing the process and ensuring the findings led to developments in practice. For example, a concern from school staff in the first two years over a perceived over-reliance on classroom observation led to a shift to focus on dialogue with staff and pupils as the main source of data collection.
- A willingness amongst the head teachers on the steering group to not 'be in charge' as they were in their own schools and to secure shared agreement over the way forward (not always easy with a group of very strong willed individuals!)
- Steering group head teachers modelling more fluid approaches to leadership and a willingness to experiment with less formally defined roles and relationships and therefore less clear accountabilities beyond their own school.
- An entrepreneurial approach to securing funding once the initial research grant had ceased and a commitment to continue funding the process from school budgets.
- Finally, an understanding of the central role of trust in the success of the collaboration was shared by all head teachers who actively constructed opportunities to build this both between themselves and across groups of staff in all partner schools.

CHAPTER 2.
The case for collaboration

The importance attached to collaboration in terms of educational policy at national level in England can be traced back to the Children's Plan (DCSF 2007). The strategies in the plan were based on five core principles of which the one most relevant in this context is the fourth:

> Services need to be shaped by and responsive to children, young people and families, not designed around professional boundaries. (p5)

Although the Children's Plan is no longer the foundation for educational policy the maxim quoted above remains true. What it does seem to point to is a greater focus on public services being designed around responsiveness and operating in a way where the quality of the service provided is more important than the historical structures and relationships informing professional relationships. In other words collaboration to provide an effective service is a higher order imperative than the internal logic of what are often described as professional silos. This principle came to be embedded in the White Paper (DCSF 2009a) *Your child, your schools, our future: building a 21st century schools system:*

> No school can meet the needs of all its pupils alone. Schools offer more by working together than any one partner could alone and to provide better value for money. At the same time, federation and other partnership solutions will become central to tackling underperformance and extending the reach of the best leaders.
>
> In order to support this approach, and to make clear that as well as making sure that their own pupils benefit from partnerships, schools should contribute to the good of other pupils, we are currently legislating to require schools to collaborate and we will go further to make it clear that schools have responsibilities for children across the area as well as those on their own roll.

The broad principles set out in the White Paper no longer apply in a statutory sense but they created a very different model of school improvement - one that challenges the orthodoxy of at least 20 years – that collaboration between schools and other agencies rather than competition is the most effective way to raise standards. This remains a significant principle of strategic thinking in education.
The Coalition White Paper 'The Importance of Teaching' (Department for Education 2010) approaches collaboration from a different perspective to the principles described above but many of the essentials remain the same. The essence of the coalition's approach can be derived from the following extracts:

2.26   As part of their work, we will expect Teaching Schools to draw together outstanding teachers in an area who are committed to supporting other schools.

2.43   Some of the country's most successful head teachers have been designated National or Local Leaders of Education. The National Leaders are outstanding head teachers of outstanding schools who commit to supporting other schools. Their schools are designated National Support Schools, because as head teachers working with other schools which may be struggling, they are expected to draw on the established strengths of their own school in order to support improvement.

5.17   Schools working together leads to better results. Some sponsors already oversee several Academies in a geographical group, or chains of Academies across the country,

7.6   We will expect schools to set their own improvement priorities. . . We will make sure that they have access to appropriate data and information so that they can identify other schools from which they might wish to learn, that there is a strong network of highly effective schools they can draw on for more intensive support, and that schools can identify other useful forms of external support as necessary.

7.13   We will also establish a new collaboration incentive worth £35m each year. This will financially reward schools which support weaker schools to demonstrably improve their performance while also improving their own.

From the Coalition's perspective collaboration is very much focused on what they perceive to be the core purpose of school improvement strategies – closing the gap between the most and least successful in the English education system. The Coalition views collaboration as the most effective strategy to support school improvement and transformation, by direct intervention, sharing best practice or collaborating through professional development.

While it may have particular application in support of education policy collaboration is the basis of civic society; it is the means by which community functions and it is fundamental to every successful human relationship. Every human endeavour will ultimately require some degree of collaboration; human social activity is posited on varying degrees of cooperation, collaboration and so interdependence. Paradoxically it seems that the best way to pursue self-interest is to cooperate in order to enable collaboration:

> A good example of the fundamental problem of cooperation is the case where two industrial nations have erected trade barriers to each other's exports. Because of the mutual advantages of free trade, both countries would be better off if these barriers were eliminated. But if either country were to unilaterally eliminate its barriers, it would find itself facing terms of trade that would hurt its own economy. (Axelrod 1984:7)

It's the classic playground confrontation "I'll let go if you let go first." What has to be recognised is that individual advantage is often found in mutual advantage but it takes joint action to achieve the optimum situation. The classic formulation of this is the concept of the prisoner's dilemma, how do individuals work out the implications of the various permutations of choosing to cooperate or not to cooperate? The alternatives are stark; either we both win or one of us loses. Now in a football match or any other sporting event in the long run, frankly, who cares? In the case of the safety, well-being and life chances of children surely the issues are too significant to leave to the vagaries of chance. In his study of cooperation as an evolutionary force Axelrod (1984:173) is optimistic about the capacity of cooperation to become embedded into a social situation:

> The main results of Cooperation Theory are encouraging. They show that cooperation can get started by even a small cluster of individuals who are prepared to reciprocate cooperation, even in a world where no one else will cooperate. The analysis also shows that the two key requisites for cooperation to thrive are that cooperation will be based on reciprocity and that the shadow of the future is important enough to make this reciprocity stable.

Cooperation, and so collaboration, can thus be described in terms of individuals making a moral choice and opting to interact in a certain way in the long term. This is, essentially, the basis of moral life – exercising a conscious choice and securing long-term relationships.

There is a very clear moral case for collaboration; virtually every faith and moral philosophy recognizes the centrality of human interaction and engagement as the basis of every moral proposition. As Hargreaves and Fink (2006: 168) express it:

> Sustainable leadership means caring for all the people our actions and choices affect – those whom we can't immediately see as well as those whom we can. …Sustainable leadership is socially just leadership, nothing simpler, nothing less.

However there are other, very strong, arguments to be made for collaboration on the basis of successful human behaviour. Surowiecki (2004:161) offers a range of reasons why scientists collaborate based on his analysis of the international response to the SARS (better known as Bird 'Flu') crisis:

1. 'Collaboration allows scientists to incorporate many different kinds of knowledge, and to do so in an active way (rather than simply learning the information from a book). (ibid p161)

2. Collaboration makes it easier for scientists to work on interdisciplinary problems. (Ibid: 162)

3. Collaboration also works because when it works well, it guarantees a diversity of perspectives. (Ibid: 162)

4. Ultimately for a collaboration to be successful it has to make each individual scientist more productive. Scientists who collaborate with each other are more productive, often times, producing 'better' science than are individual investigators. (Ibid: 162)

5. In fact, one of the more intriguing aspects of scientific collaboration is that the more productive and better known a scientist is, the more frequently he or she works with others. (Ibid: 163)

Hargreaves (2003) identifies the benefits for educators of working in networks and collaboration:

> To transform schools so that there is yet better teaching and learning, teachers must work smarter, not harder.
>
> Today, most innovation is the activity of networked teams, not individuals.
>
> Teachers need to share good practice and transfer it rapidly.
>
> Lateral networks do this more effectively than top down hierarchies.
>
> Government needs to empower teachers to use their creativity in the task of transformation.
>
> Networks of peers feed the creative co-production of new knowledge that is the source of better professional practice and renewed professional pride. (Hargreaves 2003:5)

Another example of the power of collaboration is surely Wikipedia. One of the defining characteristics of Wikipedia is the basis on which it works is one of open collaboration:

> Within minutes of the bombs going off in the London transit system someone created a

> Wikipedia page called "7 July 2005 London bombings." The article's first incarnation was five sentences long . . . The Wikipedia page received more than a thousand edits in its first four hours of existence, as additional news came in; users added numerous pointers to traditional news sources (more symbiosis) and a list of contact numbers. . (Shirky 2008: 116)

Changes in information technology and, crucially changes in the way that we perceive the role and place of technology place an even greater premium on collaboration. In Charles Leadbeater's view of a rapidly changing world the notion of We-Think becomes an essential characteristic. He defines We-Think as ' . . . how we think, play, work and create together, en masse, thanks to the web.' (Leadbeater 2008: 19)

> We-Think emerges when diverse groups of independent individuals collaborate effectively. It is not group-think: submersion in a homogeneous, unthinking mass. Crowds and mobs are as stupid as they are wise. It all depends on how the individual members combine participation and collaboration, diversity and shared values, independence of thought and community. (Ibid: 23)

In the natural world there are numerous examples of animals coordinating their behaviour to mutual benefit. Wildebeest crossing a river en masse and sardines forming a protective ball are examples of instinctive collaborative behaviour.

> A striking example of collective motion in the animal world is to be seen at dusk above the treetops as flocks of starlings swoop and dive this way and that in near –miraculous close formation. No individual is calling then shots – there is no leader. Yet every bird seems to make the same decision at the same time. (Ball 2004:151)

We-Think and Wikipedia provide powerful models of a new model of working in which the fundamental premise is one of collaboration reinforced by openness and integrated approaches. Surowiecki (2004) reinforces the capacity for collaboration that exists in many contexts even though people can be " naïve, unsophisticated agents' (ibid: 107) they can:

> Coordinate themselves to achieve complex, mutually beneficial ends, even if they're not really sure, at the start, what those ends are or what it will take to accomplish them. (Ibid: 107)

The movement towards collaboration, like any human relationship, cannot be predicted with absolute confidence but it does seem that optimism and good faith will go a long way towards making it happen. It is also important to stress the positive outcomes that are potentially available.

In very practical terms it seems reasonable to argue for the following potential benefits of collaboration between schools:

1. Standards are likely to rise as the result of the dissemination of best practice – 'closing the gap' is more achievable through collaboration.

2. There is the potential for significant economies of scale in economic terms.

3. Shared CPD has the potential to enhance consistent practice and embed improvement.

4. Strategic planning is more likely to be effective through collaborative governance.

5. Integration across phases is likely to enhance the learning experience of pupils through integrated and collective approaches.

6. Intervention to support pupils would be more effective with consistent record keeping, monitoring and use of data.

7. Deployment of staff could be more flexible and effective.

8. The potential for successful collaboration with other agencies would be significantly enhanced.

Reflection and review

1. What, in your experience, are the most compelling arguments for collaboration?
2. Is this a rational debate with logical outcomes?
3. What are the most compelling arguments to use against collaboration? How might they be responded to?
4. What is happening in an organization, community or network when collaboration is really making a difference?

CHAPTER 3
The barriers to collaborative working

The moral case for collaboration seems very strong and in many ways unarguable. As much as anything else it seems to speak to common sense and is expressed in many different ways across human history and across the full range of human experience. Whatever the context it does seem that we are 'better together'. Having said that there are multiple examples of the capacity of human beings to be divisive and to work against any idea of cooperation or collaboration. It is also vital to remember that caution and scepticism about collaboration is often historically justified and equally derived from entirely proper and valid concerns. There is a natural and proper caution by parents and governors when faced with requests for greater collaboration; they understandably wish to focus on 'their' school and the interests of 'their' own children and community. There are a wide range of diverse motivations that help to explain the resistance that is sometimes met to collaborative ventures. Resistance can be explained by a natural anxiety and insecurity about the unknown, apparent enlightened self-interest and the worst expressions of social and cultural xenophobia.

1. Self-legitimating bureaucratic systems.

    Every organization, community, workplace and project develops its own procedures, protocols and culture – 'the way we do things round here.' These processes can become enshrined in working norms to such an extent that they become the organization. The answer to the question "Why are we doing it this way?" is "Because this is the way we do it!"

    Bureaucracy may have its place, in complex working environments structures and agreed procedures can be very necessary. The danger is when the system assumes a life of its own, when the structures become more important than the relationships and when the core purpose is forgotten or subordinated to organizational imperatives – for example:

    > These are organizations that thrive on certainty and predictability. They are hierarchical; power emanates from the top, and control is vital at every level... They are heavily bureaucratic and rule-bound, and hence inflexible. They stress the single point of view, the one best way forward. (Zohar 1997:5)

    Bureaucratic systems tend to be low in trust and work to narrow, often quantitative outcomes. They are less concerned with the development of human potential than with the attainment of what are often arbitrary outcomes and their primary criterion for success is conformity

This self-referential culture results in a failure to accept or recognize alternative perspectives of the world. This is the denial of the relevance of the experience of others, the refusal to acknowledge the relevance of research or alternative ways of thinking. It is manifested as a collective closed mind, a refusal to recognise the possible relevance of other perspectives and an unwillingness to even contemplate change.

> People who work together can develop an insular culture. As they spend time with each other to the exclusion of outsiders, they restrict the influx of new viewpoints and reinforce their own beliefs. (Hansen 2009: 51)

The other, highly negative manifestation of a self-referential culture is the rejection of critical perspectives or any challenge to the prevailing orthodoxy from the stakeholders that the organization was set up to serve. In essence clients have no voice. One of the key factors in rethinking the nature of government and the public services is challenging the tendency to see the world through silos.

2. Closed language.

This is a classic dilemma. On the one hand every community; professional group, collaborative activity needs its own language to develop effective communication and a sense of shared identity. On the other hand there is nothing as exclusive as the use of closed language as a means of creating a sense of elitism, controlling access to knowledge and deliberately excluding or marginalising certain groups. One of the most powerful examples of this is the way in which in the years following the Norman Conquest of England in 1066 traditional Saxon names disappeared within a generation – you do not name your child after the losers. Language provides a powerful indicator of changes in culture. Consider the way in which the literature on leading change and innovation in education perceives risk (fundamental to significant change) and then consider how health professionals and those concerned with safeguarding view risk from a professional perspective (to be avoided or at least minimised).

Another classic manifestation of a closed language is the use of acronyms. The final report of the Cambridge Primary Review (Alexander 2010) lists over 220 acronyms and abbreviations used in education in its introductory pages. What is the most effective way of communicating to one group is impenetrable jargon to another.

> People who do not know each other have no common frame – an understanding of each other's working habits, subtle ways of articulating something, a liking of each other, and an appreciation of each other's moods.

> Lack of a common frame may not seem like a big deal, but it is. . . Without it, people become strangers in the sense of lacking a deep understanding of how to work well together. (Hansen 2009: 62)

Closed language reinforces a closed culture and education is full of potentially competing cultures – consider the attitudes (and the implicit cultural issues) in referring to 'feeder primaries', 'mainstream education', 'lower schools' and 'non-teaching staff'.

3. Parallel accountability.

One of the key concepts in describing much of public policy making is the theory of 'disjointed Incrementalism'. This is the idea that policy is made in a fragmented, ad hoc fashion with no over arching purpose so that it becomes a series of unrelated initiatives rather than a coherent, integrated, long-term strategy. In many ways the Children's Plan was so significant because it represented one of the first attempts in education in England to move towards system coherence. One area that is not, at the time of writing, keeping up with this change is the pattern of accountability.

The most significant factor compromising effective collaboration is the lack of an integrated model that actually reflects the priorities that Children's Services are accountable for. Each strand that contributes to the provision of services for children and young people continues to operate within its own model of accountability. There is no over-arching model that integrates and unites all of the elements involved in the provision of services. For example there is a very strong case for arguing that the concept of well-being should be central to any analysis of the effectiveness of provision. However the current classically incremental approach means that the accountability model is being gradually and randomly integrated where, in fact, it could be one of the most powerful tools for securing cooperation and collaboration. A shared model of well-being in childhood could serve as a powerful unifying force and as the basis for concrete collaboration. Without such a model the full potential for collaboration will always be compromised.

Accountability in English education remains essentially disjointed in two important respects. Firstly, it remains focused on the performance of the individual school rather than the network, cluster or federation and so inhibits, if not actually compromising the imperative to collaborate. Secondly the publication of school performance as league tables can only exacerbate the competitive culture. If collaboration is really going to work then a new model of accountability will be necessary; one which is based on joint responsibility for shared outcomes and focused on the well-being of the child across all agencies and services.

4. Competing professional identities.

Again there is a real dilemma here. One the one hand professional pride and a shared sense of professional identity are fundamental to any successful enterprise. On the other hand the potential exclusivity of professional status can significantly compromise possible collaboration. A very simple example is the albeit increasingly rare use in schools of the label 'non-professional' or 'non-teacher'. We would challenge anyone who has used the latter phrase to go into a hospital and ask to talk to a non-doctor when they want to talk to a nurse.

There are similar issues in terms of perceived relative status between the so-called professions.

> Status-gaps run both ways: high-status people do not want to sully their image of themselves, and low-status people do not want to let high-status people make them regret their circumstances. Both attitudes create a barrier to collaboration. (Hansen 2009: 53)

Examples of competing identities can be found in almost every walk of life and there is a real dilemma in balancing the very necessary sense of personal and professional identity with the need to engage effectively with others. Of course this blocking behaviour might well be masking personal insecurity as well as professional defensiveness. This area reinforces the centrality of the emotional responses to change in general and collaboration in particular.

5. Competition for status and resources.

This is the harsh political reality; resources are scarce, control of resources gives power and, in the final analysis organizational life is about the competition for power and control of resources of whatever type. This can be about budgets, buildings and the 'ownership' of people. In many ways this is the world of the Renaissance court transferred to the corporate headquarters, County Hall or the Town Hall or even the school. The central issue of this behaviour is what is often referred to as zero-sum or win-lose situations. At the time of writing the Copenhagen conference on climate change seems to have been dominated by zero-sum thinking rather than a win-win approach.

Transactional leadership is a common manifestation of this situation. In essence transactional leadership is descriptive of the bargaining that characterize organizational life; it sees work as a form of market place "What can I offer you to support me?" "If I do x for you will you do y for me?" Transactional leadership is largely driven by extrinsic motivation and is very much a function of status, hierarchy and the personal use (and abuse) of power. It is manifested in coalitions, secret understandings, obligations and 'offers that can't be refused'. There is a real danger that collaboration might degenerate into conspiracy if there is not a very sense of the moral nature of leadership and the importance of leaders modelling appropriate behaviours.

It is perhaps a sad, and possibly naïve, reflection on human nature that competition for scarce or finite resources always seems to precede collaboration. However it is also important to acknowledge that resistance to collaboration may be founded on real concerns about viability, the historic success of individual institutions and concern about the potential impact on jobs. It is equally important to recognise that the imperative to collaborate is often recognition of the inappropriateness of competition.

6. The territorial imperative

This is, again, a problematic and contradictory aspect of working in organizations. From one perspective a very powerful sense of identity reinforced by a collective sense of territory and the 'ownership' of space is fundamental to any community. This is the process known as bonding in social capital theory and it is the basis of every successful school, army unit, and sports team; it creates a powerful sense of belonging.

The concept of the territorial imperative comes from the natural world and is a way of explaining the social behaviour of many animals – notably the higher mammals but also many species of insect, fish and bird. For many mammals, including man, the search for territory, its subsequent appropriation and then its defence against all-comers are the dominant shared social activity and the key function of dominant, alpha, animals. Across the world the average day of the alpha female Meerkat, the alpha couple in a wolf pack and numerous executives in businesses (not to mention managers in the public sector) is spent in marking out and defending their territory in a variety of unpleasant ways.

It is this aspect of human behaviour that probably explains gang culture and many of the negative connotations of tribalism. It does seem to be the case that it is much easier to defend than to share territory and resources. There are of course some remarkable exceptions to this, notably ants and bees and, of course, dolphins and the higher primates have displayed astonishing examples of collaborative action. The territorial imperative is also a manifestation of a sense of duty and obligation, recognition of mutual responsibility and the nurturing of a sense of belonging and identity.

It would be naïve in the extreme to pretend that these obstacles to collaboration will be overcome through any sort of rational process. One of the defining and unifying factors linking the six points above is their essentially subjective and emotional nature. The various elements identified above can all be seen as natural and normal expressions of the 'real' world and as the sorts of behaviour that is responsible for success in many social environments – notably politics and life in large and complex organizations. The six elements are often mutually reinforcing and their potential negative impact is exacerbated by their complex interactions. But perhaps even more important than the political is the emotional aspect of resistance to collaboration. This is understandable, we all value being at home because we have created a world that works on our terms, we feel secure and in control. Having people to stay, however welcome, is often a strain because our world order is disrupted, normal patterns are disturbed and the usual rhythms dislocated. For many people collaboration represents the worst-case scenario in terms of disruption and dislocation. Inevitably this leads to defence mechanisms such as avoidance and flight, attack and dependency and helplessness.

Leadership strategies have to work with the emotional and non-rational at least as much as on the strategic and rational.

Reflection and review

1. Do you recognise the barriers discussed in this section from your own experience? Would you agree with our definition of them?
2. What do you perceive to be the most significant barriers working in your context?
3. What would you see as the most difficult negative attitudes to challenge and change?

CHAPTER 4
Models of collaboration

In the diagram below the potential levels of collaboration are shown as a changing balance between institutional autonomy and the extent to which that autonomy is gradually inhibited by the more formalised structures and relationships of a federation. As in any relationship there are degrees or levels of engagement – so with collaboration between schools and other agencies. As in any human relationship the movement from autonomy to collaboration involves increasing levels of openness, disclosure, trust, sharing and interdependence. It is the same as the movement from an informal acquaintance to a deep friendship. The same is true of political alliances between countries – from a low-level alliance to effective integration of economies, defence arrangements etc.

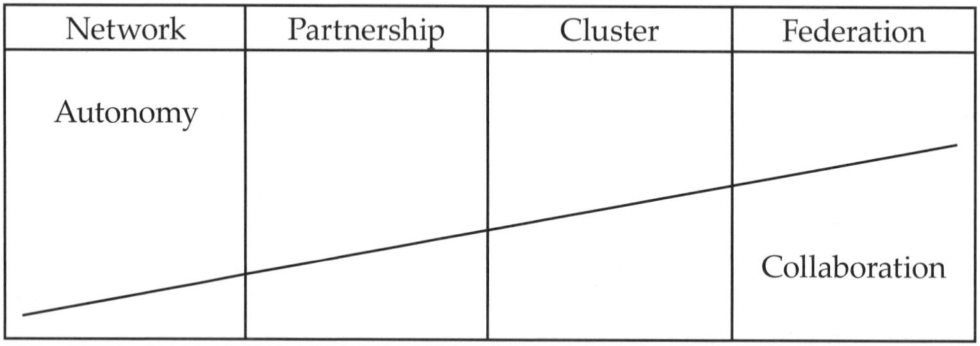

Network	Partnership	Cluster	Federation
Autonomy			Collaboration

Fig. 1: Levels of institutional engagement

A network may be defined as an informal, voluntary association that is focused on a particular strategy or area of common interest that has no implications in terms of internal school structures or formal accountability. Networks involve collaboration only to the extent of a particular project or a local strategy that emerges from mutual advantage.

A partnership is usually linked to the emerging patterns and provision of children's services at local level. Partnerships will often be the local operational provision of the Children's Trust. In particular trust and partnerships may be concerned with cross agency strategies to:

- Provide effective support to vulnerable children based on early identification and prevention via intervention.
- Develop effective and resilient families.

- Enhance young people's personal effectiveness and capacity to make valid life choices.
- Develop the skills and strategies necessary to enable economic independence.
- Reduce the levels of deprivation.
- Enhance life chances and well-being through enhancing achievement.

A cluster is a more formal and structured relationship in which there is a clear merging and integration of a number of school roles and functions, sharing of services and staff and collaboration on innovations or policy initiatives. However this does not in any way change the legal identity of the school or the formal requirements for leadership and governance.

- An integrated continuing professional development (CPD) strategy pooling budgets, developing shared provision and integrating resources with shared administration.

There are common sense and pragmatic reasons for schools' collaboration in learning networks to achieve transformation. A proper understanding of our knowledge base reveals it to be distributed, constructed and situated in our working practices. This means that collaboration across schools is a necessity rather than an optional extra in the transformation project. (Desforges 2006: 2)

- The appointment of Family Welfare Workers across a number of schools.
- Schools sharing a SENCO and Gifted and Talented Coordinator
- A number of primary schools appointing a shared School Business Manager.

The project has helped free up head teacher time and has already saved an estimated £37,000 in one year. Savings have been identified through areas such as improved management of ICT resources, energy savings and an overhaul of finance systems. (Bannister 2010: 11)

- The development of co-headship across two schools.
- Schools appointing a fundraiser to seek income and resources from a wide range of sources.
- Collaborative working on community projects with charities, community groups and churches.

Federation is a formal change in the legal status of a number of schools so that they develop a common identity. For Young (2010: 33) the advantages of federation are:

1. A high performing school can provide considerable and sustained practical support to other schools in challenging circumstances and accelerate their progress.

2. The very effective governance of one school can benefit a number of schools.
3. Outstanding leadership in one school can help transform the leadership and performance of a number of schools.
4. Community cohesion can be increased when parents/carers in a larger geographic area share a common educational provider.

International examples of alternative approaches to collaboration include:

> Belgium (Flanders) School communities have been created as voluntary collaborative partnerships between schools.
>
> Denmark Cooperation in post-compulsory education has been promoted by the creation of administrative groups that can be set up locally or regionally to optimise their joint resources.
>
> Finland Legislative reform has enhanced school cooperation aiming to ensure integrity of students' study paths.
>
> France Partnerships have been established to ensure collaboration on student orientation, educational coherence between different types of schools, common management of shared material and human resources.
>
> Netherlands In primary education "upper management'" takes management responsibility for several schools. About 80% of primary school boards have an upper school management bureau for central management, policy and support staff.
>
> Norway There is a tendency to merge schools to form an administrative unit run by a school principal
>
> Portugal Schools are grouped together with a collective management structure. There are executive, pedagogical and administrative councils.
> (Pont et al 2008: 57)

In theory at least the ultimate expression of collaboration is integration. The case study that follows is an example of increasingly sophisticated collaborative working through increasing interdependence.

Case study: The development of a co-headship approach

This is a study of the way in which an innovative collaborative leadership model dramatically improved the fortunes of a failing primary school in South West England.

Context

The average sized primary school serves an area of above average deprivation and, after a long history of difficulties, was judged to require special measures in an inspection in June 2008. In subsequent monitoring visits, it was judged to have made inadequate progress in tackling the identified weaknesses and, following the resignation of the head teacher, the LA invited the head teacher of a local outstanding school, serving the same community, to form an executive leadership team with two other experienced local heads. The team was appointed on a temporary basis from spring 2009.

Facing the challenges

The executive leadership team consisted of an executive head and two consultant head teachers each of whom took a lead in a particular aspect of school improvement. One consultant head, interviewed for this study, took responsibility for developing teaching and learning and worked in the school two days a week. The challenges facing the team were considerable. Standards were dramatically low and expectations of pupils limited. Teaching was unsatisfactory in many lessons and behaviour management poor, resulting in a climate where many children reported not feeling completely safe. Many essential systems and structures did not seem to be in place and the school was facing significant financial challenges.

Although the members of the team did not know each other well before taking on the challenge, the severity of the difficulties faced demanded high levels of trust to be established very quickly, with decisions made by each member being fully supported by all from the outset. Because each member was not on site every day, phone calls and text messages formed a central plank of daily communication.

The team secured the services of the LA senior HR officer one day a week, and this expertise, along with the high level of mutual trust and support within the team, enabled them to tackle the significant staffing challenges robustly including quality assuring the high number of supply teachers required during long periods of staff turbulence.

The governing body was dissolved and replaced by an Interim Executive Board (IEB) with extensive experience and a high level of skill. The IEB worked in close partnership with the executive team, both in supporting them in the many difficult challenges they faced and ensuring clear lines of communication with staff and parents were maintained. An example of this was the establishment of a parent forum to offer reassurance and deal with inevitable parental concerns.

Distributing leadership: the case for co-headship

Following subsequent HMI monitoring visits indicating that the school was now starting to make clear progress, the executive team and the IEB were keen to establish a sustainable solution to the leadership challenge at the school. It was agreed to create a co-headship model consisting of the one of the executive team consultant heads who was head of the neighbouring outstanding school, and her deputy. A management partnership was created in which both act as joint head teachers across the two schools. This joint headship model took effect from January 2010.

Governors at the outstanding school were happy to support this model as it enabled them to retain their very experienced head teacher and also the deputy, who, due to the development experiences offered through the challenges may well have moved on to a headship opportunity elsewhere. The co-head team had already demonstrated a strong proven working relationship, high levels of creative thinking and problem solving, extensive leadership experience and expertise and inside knowledge of the locality and needs of both schools.

The commitment to making this model possible was shared by the LA legal and HR teams along with Governors, the IEB and the head teachers, as they worked to solve the considerable legal complexities around contractual arrangements. This tenacity and determination to find solutions to problems faced is a feature of the leadership described in this study.

Between January and March 2010 the co-heads worked hard to secure a real partnership between the two schools, building on the strong links established during the executive leadership team tenure. Joint INSET days have taken place, the schools share the services of the established School Business Manager, subject leaders have started to work closely across both schools and several staff have had opportunities to shadow teachers in the outstanding school.

Outcomes

In March 2010 the failing school was again visited by HMI and this time, both removed from special measures and judged to be good overall, with leadership deemed outstanding.

'The exceptional vision and drive, established by the executive leadership team, are shared and maintained to a very high standard by the co-head teachers. The interim executive board has made an outstanding contribution to school improvement…

The close relationship with XX school is having a positive impact on the professional development of teachers.'
Ofsted 2010

Sustainability

Both the schools in the partnership have appointed new deputy heads and the job responsibilities of both have been fully aligned as part of a structure of four-way support. There is a clear succession plan in place with the professional development opportunities provided for all senior staff in both schools structured to benefit from the shared expertise.

The highly successful three head teacher executive leadership team model has been adopted by the LA, who, aware of the factors that contributed to success in this instance, are deploying the approach in another failing school.

Implications for leadership for collaboration

The co-head teacher interviewed for this study identified the following as being significant when working in a collaborative executive team or a co –headship model.

- *A licence to be radical in approaches and solutions, facilitated by the full support of the LA, the creativity of the heads and the fact that, in the words of one of the heads 'it could not have got any worse'.*
- *A high level of collaboration with the LA including aligning School Improvement Partners, dedicated support from HR and legal services*
- *High levels of trust between executive team members and subsequently the co-head teachers*
- *Actively building the trust of staff and parents through transparent communication, targeting appropriate staff members for praise and high levels of personal credibility given the track record of the three heads teachers*
- *A clear understanding of the management of change including the emotional impact on individuals and the school community*
- *A clear division of roles and responsibilities both during the executive team period and the co-headship, with a commitment to capitalise on shared development opportunities*
- *A tenacity and determination to overcome all challenges to improve outcomes of all pupils in the shared community*
- *Acting as advocates for the benefits of collaboration between the two schools, highlighting the gains to be made for both.*

Reflection and review

1. Do your experiences of collaborative working confirm or deny the points made in this chapter?
2. What other possibilities exist for collaboration between schools?
3. What are the perceptions of different types of collaboration across your school community?

CHAPTER 5
Strategies for effective collaboration

The benefits of collaboration do seem to outweigh any negatives time after time. While autonomy is a natural human imperative the lesson of the porcupines is generally well understood and that in order to collaborate effectively:

> . . . we don't have to surrender our individuality. In nature, good decision-making comes as much from competition as from compromise, from disagreement as much as from consensus . . . we add something of value to the team or organization mainly by bringing something authentic and original to the table. (Miller 2010: 268)

Miller (ibid:267) identifies a number of simple principles that seem to explain the success of collaborative communities in nature:

- A reliance on local knowledge – which maintains a diversity of information
- The application of simple rules of thumb – which minimizes computational needs
- Repeated interactions among group members – helping to amplify faint but important signals and speed up decision making.
- The use of quorum thresholds – too improve the accuracy of decisions
- A healthy dose of randomness in individual behaviour – to keep a group from getting stuck in problem-solving ruts

As in any successful human relationship, effective collaboration seems to be getting the balance right between the individual and the group and then ensuring that certain basic principles are in place.

1. Transformational leadership.

    If the barriers to collaboration identified in the previous section are to be systemically and systematically challenged then, at the very least, leadership of the change process will have to be transformative. According to Atwater and Atwater (1994: 151)

    > Incrementalist strategies apply when the organization's methods basically fit its current and predicted environment Radical transformational strategies are necessary when the organization is markedly out of fit with the demands of its environment

    Previous sections have sought to demonstrate that the demands of collaborative strategies mean that schools and other agencies are seriously 'out of fit' with the environment. O'Sullivan (1999:4) expresses the tension thus:

> When any cultural manifestation is at its zenith, the educational and learning tasks are uncontested and the culture is of one mind about what is ultimately important. There is, during these periods, a kind of optimism and verve that ours is the best of all possible worlds and we should continue what we are doing.

O'Sullivan goes on to distinguish between educational reform as working within the prevailing system and 'transformative criticism' which 'suggests a radical restructuring of the dominant culture and a fundamental rupture with the past.' (Ibid: 5) Taffinder reinforces this perspective (1998:36)

> Transformation attacks both the current and the known world and the future. It is concerned with the creation of new opportunities, with the ability to junk conventional wisdom and destroy old (often cherished) advantages, to violate established business practice, compete in different ways, shut down competitors' angle of attack and behave in counterintuitive and, indeed, unpredictable ways.

'Junking conventional wisdom' is one of the most powerful manifestations of transformative thinking – it is the junking rather than the enhancing of conventional wisdom that really begins to mark out the transformative approach. Challenging the orthodoxies that were described in the previous section is a fundamentally transformative act. Taffinder (ibid:38) goes on to make the point that 'more is invested in the past than in the future' – in many ways transformation is about reversing that relationship. Hock (1999:9) reinforces this point:

> Every mind is a room filled with archaic furniture. It must be moved about or cleared away before anything new can enter. This means ruthless confrontation of the many things we know that are no longer so.

For Coleman (2008:3) the success factors relevant to leadership for collaboration would include:

> Context: awareness of history, population and politics
>
> Membership relations: communication, trust and trustworthiness, power and status
>
> Culture and language: communications, professional language, trust

> Structures: formal and informal
>
> Planning and resources: skill and expertise, finances, resource constraints
>
> Vision, aims and objectives: clarity of aims, moral purpose.

What is clear from Coleman's analysis is that leadership for collaboration is the product of a very complex set of highly interdependent variables and that trust is pivotal to every aspect of collaboration.

2. Shared values and vision.

> In this context, values is taken to mean the moral purpose that acts as the key foundation for all collaborative activities. In essence values serve as the unifying factor that integrates and prioritises all decision making and planning. Vision is essentially the description of the preferred future for which the particular network, cluster, partnership or federation exists. What does appear to be fundamental to any successful move towards collaboration is the identification of values and vision that transcend previous historical identities – rather in the way that the great nation-states emerged in the nineteenth century and created a super ordinate sense of identity. For Hargreaves and Fink (2006: 158) the moral consensus in education has to move from the historical preoccupation with the individual school to a much broader concern that transcends traditional boundaries and relationships:
>
>> The hardest part of sustainable leadership is the part that provokes us to think beyond our own schools and ourselves. It is the part that calls us to serve the public good of all people's children within and beyond our community and not only the private interests of those who subscribe to our own institution.

3. High trust.

> Trust is fundamental to collaboration; in fact it is impossible to think of collaboration without linking it to the level of trust existing between the various parties involved. There are numerous ways of defining trust in leadership but the following elements would seem to be fundamental to any useful definition:
>
> - Credibility – levels of integrity and authenticity
> - Consistency – reliability over time
> - Competence – demonstrated professional expertise

Taken together these elements would point to confidence in a person, an organization a service or a product. If collaboration is to work then it has to be rooted in trust, which means building consistency, credibility, and competence and so confidence.

Historically trust has tended to be seen as a quality found within an organization rather than as a quality between organizations working in the same sphere. An alternative, but related, approach is found in the emerging theory of wikinomics, in which the key principle is collaboration:

> …The new promise of collaboration is that with peer production we will harness human skill, ingenuity, and intelligence more efficiently and effectively than anything we have witnessed previously. Sounds like a tall order. But the collective knowledge, capability, and resources embodied within broad horizontal networks of participants can be mobilized to accomplish much more than one firm acting alone. (Tapscott & Williams 2006: 18)

Tapscott and Williams identify four principles of Wikinomics:

Being open: In essence this is about collaboration and sharing; maximizing the transfer of ideas and innovation, it is another manifestation of Leadbeater's model of We-think.

Peering: Wikinomics is non-hierarchical; it invites involvement and openness and is based on self-organization rather than hierarchical control models. Peering encourages participations from any source and respects the value of all ideas, irrespective of the status of their originator.

Sharing: involves the end of copyright and patents allowing for shared improvement and the development of ideas, projects and strategies.

Acting globally: means moving beyond the parochial and interacting with a far larger community than ever before.

This might all seem very utopian but Tapscott and Williams start with the story of a gold mining company in economic difficulties that broke the fundamental taboo of the industry by publishing all its geological data on the internet and asking for advice on where to mine for gold – and offering a reward. The turnover of the company increased from $100 million to $9 billion – almost entirely because of openness, collaboration and trust. According to Coleman (2008: 14) trust is fundamental to collaboration for the following reasons:

- Trust was seen to improve performance including improved levels of functionality and increased competence.
- Trust also acted as a means of reducing mistakes by increasing confidence and reducing fear of errors, encouraging individuals to see them as learning opportunities.
- Trust supported the development of relationships and helped to overcome competition and suspicion, especially where this stemmed from a lack of familiarity.
- Trust directly benefited collaboration by supporting communication.
- The presence of trust made it easier to discuss sensitive issues openly.

4. Multiple interdependent networks

Any form of collaboration seems more likely to be successful if it is seen as a form of network with multiple interconnecting strands. It is in this complexity that the full potential of collaboration can be realised; however it would be naïve to pretend that networks can be self-managing and sustaining. In some circumstances they can be, but this is probably only possible in optimum situations. Normally the management of collaborative relationships requires certain criteria to be met if they are to be successful and sustainable. They need to be:

- Manageable in terms of scope and purpose.
- Responsive to community need.
- Structured to maximise efficient and cost-effective operations.
- Geographically proximate to facilitate communication.
- Designed to create a critical mass to maximise impact.
- Led to maximise engagement and collaboration.

5. Bonding to bridging

The fates of Easter Island and the settlement on Greenland described in the introduction can be best understood in terms of Putnam's (2002) related concepts of bonding and bridging. Bonding describes the circumstances in which a community develops a sense of its distinctive identity; its differences to other communities and an awareness of its potential uniqueness. Putnam describes bonding as the 'superglue' that binds a community together. Bonding is expressed through the sense of identity of community members, the homogeneity of the community and the introversion of the community.

Bridging, by contrast is the 'WD40' that enables communities to engage with other communities. Bridging refers to the capacity to find common cause, to communicate and to explore the possibility of interdependent working. Bridging is thus concerned with inclusion and shared communication.

The civilization on Easter Island and the settlement in Greenland both collapsed because the imperatives to bond were stronger that the imperatives to bridge. At the heart of successful collaboration is the ability to transfer the cultural and historical focus on bonding to a focus on bridging.

6. Participative projects.

What seems to be essential in developing collaborative approaches is a focus on action rather than consultation and planning. All the evidence indicates that the best way to develop a collaborative culture is to actually engage in collaborative activities.

In his study of successful strategies to renew and enhance communities Putnam (2003:294) identifies a range of common criteria:

- Careful analysis of the 'structural conditions', for example the availability of resources from a range of sources and the application of existing policies and strategies to underpin a community initiative.
- The use of federation, 'nesting' smaller groups within larger groups to develop sophisticated interdependent networks to enhance a sense of belonging, commitment and to foster personal relationships.
- Fostering engagement and commitment by developing an overarching and shared sense of belonging through common purpose and shared values.
- Recognize the need for ownership through the development and respect for peoples own stories, build the capacity for dialogue through valuing personal and collective narratives.
- Building multi stranded networks of shared interest and common concern that utilize a wide range of communication technologies.
- 'Reweaving social webs will depend in part on the efforts of dedicated local leaders who choose to pursue their goals…through the sometimes slow, frequently fractious, and profoundly transformative route of social capital building. But reweaving will also depend on our ability to create new spaces for recognition, reconnection, conversation and debate.'

7. Building community capacity/distributed leadership

A common characteristic of hierarchical organizations in which the culture is one based in bonding is that leadership tends to be related to personal status and is often an expression of personality. This factor is often cited as a major barrier to developing collaborative working and a key element in the failure of collaborative ventures. The issue appears to be the need to move from a view of leadership as personal status to seeing leadership as collective capacity that is not linked to role, status, age or experience.

8. Open accountability.

If collaboration is really to work then the current pattern of accountability will have to change. In terms of the education system the current pattern might be described as a closed system. It is closed because it a/ works on a very narrow view of what accountability should focus on i.e. academic performance and b/ it is very personal to the head teacher and the school. It is now well established that school performance is the result of a wide range of complex variables and this should be reflected in the pattern of accountability. If collaborative working is to become the norm the accountability model should reflect this as was indicated on page 37

9. Collaboration - monitoring, review, evaluation and accountability.

Any project which seeks to develop and enhance collaboration of any sort must build in strategies to review and evaluate the success or otherwise of the project in order to demonstrate and model appropriate levels of accountability.
Criteria for the effective review and evaluation of collaboration

- Demonstrated understanding of core purpose and evidence of engagement.
- Pupil voice and the voice and perceptions of significant stakeholders.
- Recognition of each stakeholder's potential contribution and relative impact.
- Agreement of a clear hierarchy of significance of variables.
- Calibration of relative significance.
- Quantitative indicators where appropriate – monitoring through data, making judgements based on review, measuring impact through evaluation.

Strategies to measure impact

- Explicit and specific targets.
- Clear purpose and explicit expectations, focused initiatives, agreed priorities.
- Definition and agreement of relevant success criteria.
- A clear understanding of outstanding pedagogy and how that relates to standards and outcomes.
- Consistency and teacher alignment on validity of strategies.

- Leadership focused on outcomes for the child.
- Recognition of the importance of context and relative perspectives.
- Negotiation to identify and employ data that is fit for purpose.
- Relate the review model to effective learning strategies.

Any approach to evaluation that seeks to measure impact needs to use an approach similar to the model below (or one similar) in order to ensure systematic and consistent approaches to review and evaluation:

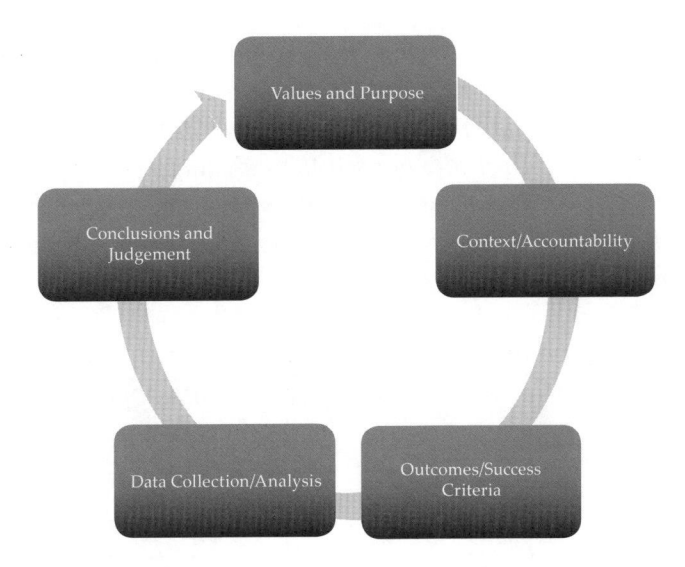

Fig. 2: An integrated approach to monitoring, review and evaluation.

Principles to inform measuring impact.

1. Success criteria need to be few in number and clearly focused; danger of dilution.
2. Tension between top down and bottom up priorities and targets.
3. Restricted amount of meaningful data available at local level.
4. Aspects of well-being very difficult to measure e.g. happiness.
5. 'We must measure what we value, not value what we can easily measure.'
6. The need to reconcile existing accountability models with moral purpose.
7. The need for a 'menu' of strategies to suit local contexts.
8. Relating findings to appropriate action.

9. Relating findings to appropriate interventions.
10. Quality outcomes the result of quality processes.
11. Recognition of organic nature of collaborative activities.
12. Any model must secure professional consensus.

The following case studies provide practical examples of many of the principles outlined above.

Case Study: Collaboration to support learning

As an end of year project, Year 10 learners at Peacehaven Community School planned and taught French lessons to Year 6 pupils in partner primary schools   Peacehaven Community School (PCS) is a mixed comprehensive school on the south coast of England. The majority of its pupils come from three local primary schools: Hoddern, Meridian and Telscombe Cliffs. The Year 10 students used the Personal Learning and Thinking Skills resource as the basis of their planning and they were then taught a lesson in Russian to give them the experience of learning something totally new as French would be to the primary pupils. They then planned lessons and developed resources to support their sessions in the primary school.

The four schools are committed to collaborative working and this project was seen as a way of sharing effective learning and teaching; introducing French into the primary schools and applying the learning emerging from the use of PLTS by year 10 students.

Not only did the four schools collaborate but so did students and staff with uniformly positive results:

> *'Yesterday I had the pleasure of watching some of our students demonstrate how very talented they are. I watched a small group of our Year 10 students deliver a French lesson to a mixed age Year 4/5 class at Meridian Primary School. The quality of their resources, their teaching methodology and classroom management were exceptional.'*
> *Deputy Head, Peacehaven*

> *'Our Year 6 children responded very positively to the lesson and have been asking for more! I was impressed with all the PCS students*
> *Year 5/6-teacher Hoddern Junior School*

> *'It was fun and we played games'. 'I learnt all the colours and I also learnt a French song to remember it!'...'My sister does French and I really want to learn more stuff about French!' ... 'Can you come again?' ... 'Can you come every week?' ... 'That was wicked!' ... 'We'll pay you to come back!'*
> *Year 6 learners*

'It provided a great opportunity for different students to work together in different situations. It has

also raised the profile of languages amongst the Key Stage 4 students as feedback from the project has been so positive.'
Head of Languages Peacehaven

'I was excited but nervous ... It gave me so much confidence in my French ... I'm quite shy but I really enjoyed doing it and feel more confident in myself ... It was amazing they listened to us ... 'We learnt how to learn ... My organisational skills have really improved ... You learn to explain yourself clearer, because they mirror everything you say ... It refreshed our memories – it was useful to re-do Year 7 stuff.'
Year 10 students Peacehaven

www.cilt.org.uk/secondary/1419/gcse/gcse_overview/case_studies/using_plts.aspx

Case study: Partnership working in East Hampshire

Michele Frost and Jackie Adams

The East Hampshire Education Improvement Partnership (EHEIP) is a partnership of maintained schools across the primary, secondary and sixth form college sectors in East Hampshire. We have a shared vision to improve the life chances and educational attainment for children and young people in our area. There are 44 of us and together we are able to achieve more than doing this alone. The East Hampshire Education Improvement Partnership exists to close gaps in educational attainment, raise standards in attainment across the board and provide joint professional development for staff and governors

- We pool resources.
- We run outstanding projects.
- We are supported by Governors.
- We work with other services that have an impact on children and young people.
- We work with the Local Children's Partnerships in our area, with the District Council and the Hampshire Children's Trust.
- We are passionate about the impact of our joint working on the future of our children and young people.

The EHEIP's aims are:

- school and post-16 improvement and raising attainment through personalisation of provision for all learners.
- overcoming barriers to learning, including behaviour and attendance, in order to deliver the outcomes of Every Child Matters, The Children's Plan and relevant aspects of The Children and

Young People's Plan (Hampshire).
- *achieving sustainability by promoting Continual Professional Development and fostering innovative leadership opportunities.*

Why have a partnership like this?

As a group of head teachers we recognised that the needs of many of our young people, particularly our vulnerable young people were not being met by our current system which was based much more around competition rather than cooperation and collaboration. Although, we did not have specific data to support our thoughts we had plenty of local data and intelligence that told us that as early 4 years of age we could potentially identify future NEETS (Not in Education, Employment or Training) even a young person who may become another statistic on the teenage pregnancy list or fail to achieve 5 A* to C at GCSE level.

A group of us met with colleagues from the local authority (LA) and interested head teachers and principals across East Hampshire with the notion of developing a partnership to address issues that we had all encountered in our different localities and schools. Like any initiative people came with mixed ideas and questions; such as What will it's function be? How will it work/look? What is in it for our school? In reality we did not know all the answers but we had the faith and passion to try something new which we believed would be effective in offering staff development, breaking down barriers between schools and providing opportunities for children that individual schools would struggle to offer alone.

We worked with the LA, especially the governor services who gave us advice on creating a memorandum of agreement and joint governance arrangements. This gave us the opportunity to make legally binding agreements and financial commitments. At the time of creating this partnership we did not realise just how important this procedure was.

We asked schools and our local college to contribute £5 per pupil; this made every schools/college contribution fair and equitable; the smallest school with a number on role of only 38 pupils whilst the largest was our college with over 2000 students. This allowed every organisation to be involved and benefit from all the opportunities on offer within the partnership. In November we appointed a EHEIP coordinator for just one day a week to seek future funding, set up a joint website and organise a joint conference for all headteachers and governors to share the partnerships achievements, plan future projects and analyse our strengths as well as any pitfalls.

This type of commitment and partnership has taken trust, shared beliefs and drive. It has also meant a change in culture amongst the organisations, a sense of shared responsibility and a very strong sense of moral purpose and social conscience. We have taken on the African motto 'It takes a whole community to raise a child'. We believe that every young person, regardless of which school he attends is part of our community, is our young citizen and therefore is our joint responsibility .We simply cannot ignore it. After all we also know that we all need to take the responsibility of reducing the number of NEETs because statistics show us that the following factors play a key role for NEETs

- *Lower life expectancy*
- *Higher family breakdown*
- *Less happy as NEET and at school before becoming NEET*
- *Unfulfilled ambition*
- *Involved in crime*
- *Increased drugs and substance misuse*

We can also recognise Pre-NEET Indicators, such as

- *Persistent truants*
- *Permanently excluded*
- *Free School Meals*
- *Disability*
- *Poor attainment*
- *Parents or young person have low aspirations*
- *Young people who have existing vulnerability, including children in care, travellers, those who have Special Needs, some children of Black and Ethnic Minority status, children of very young parents, young people involved in drugs and substance misuse, also suffer from poor emotional health.*

We equally all know

> *"poor behaviour and attainment at school leads to raised risk of unemployment, social marginality and low status, low control jobs in adult life. This pattern of poor education and employment damages health and, ultimately, cognitive function in old age."*
> *(WHO Report 2003)*

Many of these factors can also be recognised with teenage pregnancy rates as they are:

- *Less likely to finish their education, and more likely to bring up their child alone and in poverty;*
- *The infant mortality rate for babies born to teenage mothers is 60% higher than for babies born to older mothers;*
- *Teenage mothers have three times the rate of post-natal depression of older mothers and a higher risk of poor mental health for three years after the birth*

The impact on the outcomes for children of teenage parents is also a grave concern as children of teenage mothers are generally at increased risk of poverty, low educational attainment, poor housing and poor health, and have lower rates of economic activity in adult life.

We therefore need to tackle these concerns through partnerships and collaboration as we have seen that as a single individual school we cannot make the difference overall which is needed. It is our collective responsibility that will ultimately make the difference alongside a keen moral imperative.

Successes of the Partnership by June 2010

Since our formation in September 2009, the EIP has run the following projects:

- *Independent child and student initiated learning*
- *Gifted and talented young artists, writers and photographers*
- *Raising standards in writing*
- *Raising standards in mathematics*
- *New 'nurture' facility for primary children at risk of exclusion*
- *Middle leaders training*
- *Training for Emotional Literacy Support Assistants (ELSA)*
- *Working in partnership for governors*

These projects have been funded through pooled resources and grant funding from other agencies. Some of these projects have been completed and others will develop across the next academic year (2010-2011).

Next Steps and projects

The EHEIP is developing and evolving many current and new projects for the next academic year (2010-2011):

- *Raising standards in English.*
- *Raising standards in mathematics (through the development of a children and young people's business enterprise using a Dragon's Den type model with Dragon's Den as a vehicle).*
- *Improving provision for gifted and talented children and young people (including areas such as music, sport and further training for GAT Co-ordinators).*
- *Extending and developing 'nurture' provision for primary school children.*
- *Providing a new and additional facility for vulnerable secondary school children.*
- *Establishing a middle leaders' programme with a new cohort of staff.*
- *Extending ELSA training for a further 20 staff and provision of supervision for currents ELSAs.*

- *Working in partnership with governors to share expertise.*
- *Closing the gap in attainment for children and young people at most risk of underachievement, low aspirations and poor behaviour.*
- *Developing health and sex education at all levels with a particular focus on rights, respect, responsibilities and reducing the number of teenage pregnancies.*
- *Developing effective independent learning.*
- *Organising an East Hampshire Mini-Olympics working with the Sports Partnership towards a mini-Olympics for children and young people.*

Reflection and review

1. Which of the strategies outlined in this chapter are you comfortable and confident in using?
2. Which of them present a challenge?
3. Are there any approaches not mentioned in the chapter that have been successful in your experience?
4. How confident do you think your colleagues are at the prospect of working collaboratively?

CHAPTER 6
Conclusion: Leadership for collaboration

This final section identifies and integrates the key issues developed both in the discussion so and in the case studies and offers a number of core principles that seem to us to be needed to inform any approach to successful leadership for collaboration.

The fundamental rationale for collaboration is that it enables improvement and offers a range of strategies that promise high impact and high leverage, in essence more for less. Fullan (2005: 93-94) summarises the benefits:

> First, people get access to good ideas from other practitioners- ideas that are grounded and workable from respected peers who have successfully grappled with difficult problems. Second, people begin to identify with larger parts of the system beyond their narrow interest groups . . . When people get out to do something worthwhile with peers in other schools or jurisdictions, the sense of community and commitment enlarges . . . Third, if enough people get out – the collective capacity to system think, and thus to system change, is advanced.

Fullan stresses the importance of collaboration and networking not being viewed 'as ends seen as automatically good in and of themselves'. (P94) Rather they have to be seen as both effective and efficient and, crucially, reflecting moral purpose in how improvement is achieved and not just what is achieved. Leadership for collaboration involves some or most of the following in various permutations according to context.

1. All actions, policies and strategies must be underpinned by a clear moral purpose, with a high level of commitment to improving outcomes for children and young people beyond the limit of the leader's own school.

2. A commitment to distributing leadership widely in a variety of contexts and to deploying a coaching model to actively build leadership capacity is essential.

3. There needs to be the courage to take a transformational, risk- taking approach when required; a willingness to challenge orthodoxy, combined with the tenacity and determination to achieve the desired outcomes in spite of considerable challenge.

4. Collaboration requires politically intelligent leaders: an understanding of national level policy direction as well as an understanding of the local political context, a willingness to deploy this effectively such as in identifying key players in the local community and LA or significant

funding opportunities, and acting as an advocate for collaboration, regularly articulating the vision within the community.

5. Contextual intelligence means that leaders have to be committed to gaining a detailed understanding of the real needs of the community served by the collaboration and ensuring systems are in place for members of the community to have regular input into it's future direction

6. Leadership has to ensure that appropriate and sustainable systems and structures are in place so that collaborative activities remain at the heart of all the participant groups' organisational culture.

7. Leaders need to be personally comfortable with both a high level of ambiguity and undefined and constantly changing accountabilities.

8. There has to be a proactive approach to ensuring high levels of communication across the collaboration, with a particular focus on transparency and the establishment of a shared language, particularly across professional boundaries.

9. An understanding of the central role of trust in facilitating effective collaboration and the ability to both inspire trust personally as leader and to be able to build it proactively with a wide and diverse range of colleagues and members of the community.

It may be that we are seeing a fundamental rethinking of the nature of leadership in education away from school leadership into leadership across a community or system. The primary justification for this is not collaboration for its own sake but rather because:

> There is evidence that the process of change is more resilient and improvement more sustainable when school collaborate and learn from other schools. Schools that sustain improvement are usually well networked and have a good structure of internal support.
>
> While such schools may be considered to be leading the way for others to follow, the reciprocal nature of the relationship and the opportunities for schools to innovate together means there is added value in both directions from these forms of collaboration.
> (Leithwood et al 2010 P238)

Reflection and review

How would you rank yourself against each of the following criteria for leading collaboration? How would other members of your team rate you? How do you rate them?

1. Shared aims, alignment on values, clear purpose

Not Present	0	1	2	3	4	Fully Present

2. High expectations and aspirations

Not Present	0	1	2	3	4	Fully Present

3. Contextual awareness and sensitivity – high engagement

Not Present	0	1	2	3	4	Fully Present

4. Agreed future scenarios – a shared view of a preferred future

Not Present	0	1	2	3	4	Fully Present

5. Widely distributed leadership, systematic capacity building

Not Present	0	1	2	3	4	Fully Present

6.   Openness, transparency and personal accountability

Not Present	0	1	2	3	4	Fully Present

7.   Project based learning and working – changing through doing

Not Present	0	1	2	3	4	Fully Present

8.   Emphasis on high quality working relationships – consensus building

Not Present	0	1	2	3	4	Fully Present

9.   Opportunities for achievement

Not Present	0	1	2	3	4	Fully Present

10.   Systematic monitoring, review and evaluation

Not Present	0	1	2	3	4	Fully Present

What are the implications of your scores for you, your team and the school?

References

Alexander, R. (Ed) (2010) Children, their World, their Education London, Routledge (The Cambridge Primary Review)

Atwater, L.E. and Atwater, D.C. (1994) 'Organizational Transformation: Strategies for Change and Improvement', in Bass, B.M and Avolio, B.J. (1994)

Axelrod A (1984) The Evolution of Cooperation London Penguin Books

Ball P (2004) Critical Mass London Arrow Books

Bannister N (2010) Collaborate and thrive, Ldr, March 2010, Issue 38

Bass, B.M and Avolio, B.J. (1994) Improving Organizational Effectiveness Through Transformational Leadership, London: Sage

Buonfino, A., and Mulgan, G. (2006) Porcupines in Winter, London: The Young Foundation

Coleman A (2008) Trust in Collaborative Working, Nottingham NCSL

DCSF (2007) The Children's Plan

DCSF (2009a) Your child, your schools, our future: building a 21st century schools system. The White Paper

DCSF (2009b) Your Child, Your School, Our Future: Timetable for action – Primary Schools

Department for Education (2010) The Importance of Teaching The White Paper

Desforges C (2006) Collaboration for transformation: why bother? Nottingham NCSL

Diamond J (2005) Collapse: How Societies Choose to Fail or Survive London Allen Lane

Hansen M (2009) Collaboration Boston Ma Harvard Business Press

Hargreaves, A. and Fink, D. (2006): Sustainable Leadership San Francisco Jossey Bass

Hargreaves D (2003) Education Epidemic London Demos

Leadbeater C (2008) We-Think London Profile Books

Leithwood K Harris A and Strauss T (2010) Leading School Turnaround San Francisco Jossey Bass

Miller P (2010) Smart Swarm London Collins

O'Sullivan, E. (1999) Transforming Leaning: Educational Vision for the 21st Century, London: Zed Books

Pont, B. Nusche, D. and Moorman, H. (2008) Improving School Leadership Volume1 Paris OECD

Putnam, R. (2003) Better Together, New York, Simon and Schuster

Shirky C (2008) Here Comes Everybody London Penguin

Surowiecki J (2004) The wisdom of Crowds London, Little Brown

Taffinder, P. (1998) Big Change, Chichester: John Wiley

Tapscott D. And Williams, A.D. (2006) Wikinomics London: Atlantic Books

Young M (2010) First steps to federation, Ldr, March 2010, Issue 38

Zohar D (1997) Rewiring the Corporate Brain San Francisco Berrett-Koehler